T0198426

# Maria Khan Villava

# Mommy, Your Kisses Make Me A Winner

To order additional copies of this book, contact:
Xlibris
844-714-8691
www.Xlibris.com
Orders@Xlibris.com

ISBN:    Softcover        978-1-6641-8121-2
         EBook            978-1-6641-8120-5

Print information available on the last page

Rev. date: 06/18/2021

This book is dedicated to
my forever sonshine, Sean.

Always remember that you can achieve
anything you set your heart out to do.
I love you to infinity and beyond!

It was a warm bright sunny afternoon. Mommy and Sean were gathering his baseball belongings for his big game. He was very excited but also nervous at the same time.

Sean was a part of the Little Angels baseball team. As he was preparing, he asked, "Mommy what if I don't win the game today?" Mommy then replied, "Just try your very best, but no matter the outcome, you'll always be a winner in my eyes." They both smiled and hugged one another and off they went.

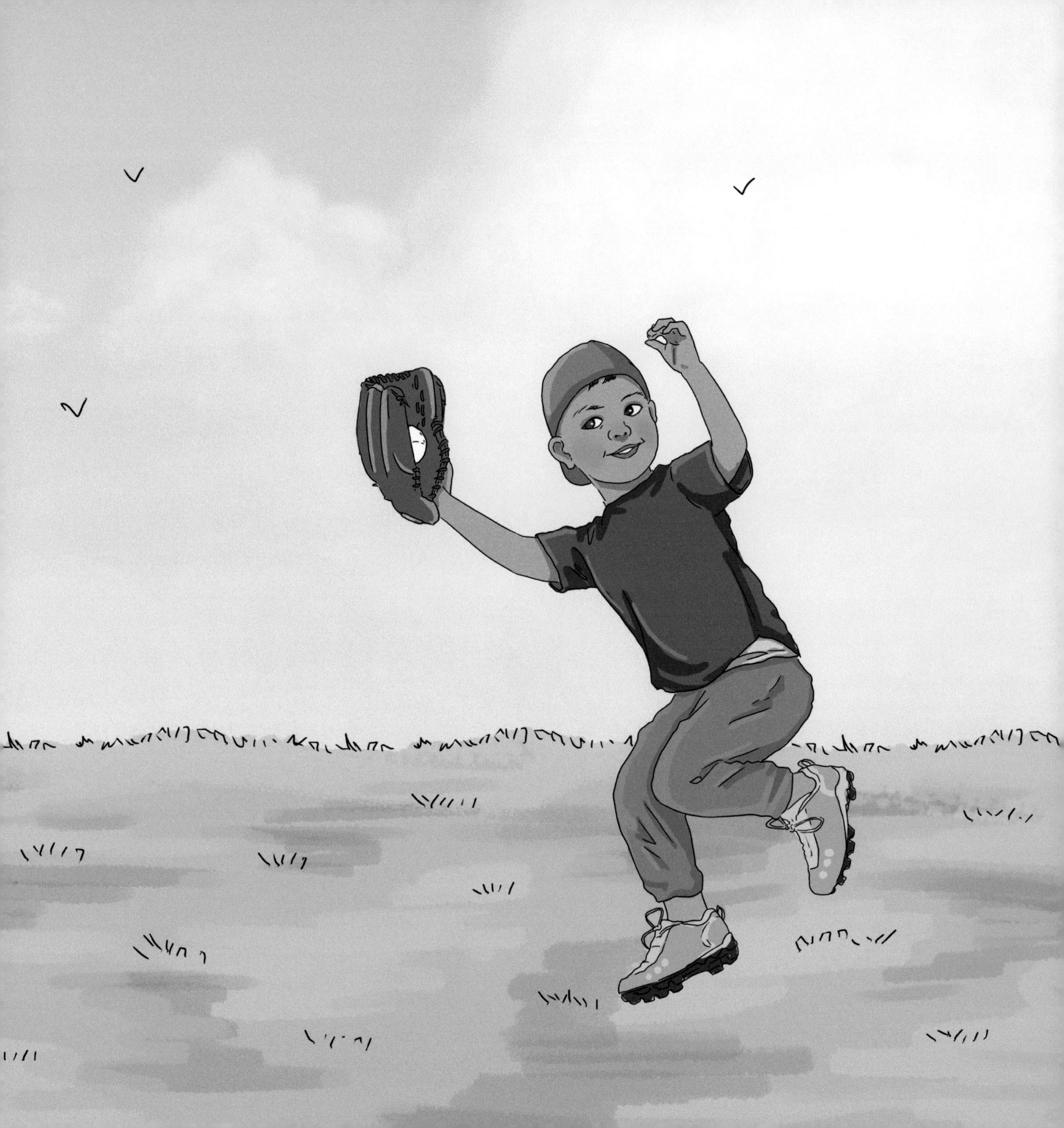

All the players were present and ready to play. As Mommy waited out on the sideline, she waved and blew Sean a kiss. He had the biggest smile. Standing in position, he was ready to conquer the game and finish it with a win.

You can hear all cheers and encouragement coming from both teams. Parents, families, and siblings were all excited. The coaches were determined to help their baseball team win.

"Go, go, go, run, you can do this" chanted the parents. And to Mommy's surprise, they announced the winning team, Little Angel's. Mommy was so excited she was jumping up and down.

Sean came running as fast as he could to Mommy. He hugged her so tight and said, "Mommy your kisses make me a winner!" Mommy was so happy and she kissed little Seanie back and said, "In my eyes, you'll always be my winner."

Off they went to enjoy a nice afternoon lunch with Sean, Mommy, and his family. They enjoyed a nice meal of pancakes, steak, and eggs. And together they all said, "We Knew You Could Do It!"

Later that evening, Mommy kissed Sean and said, you can achieve anything you put your heart and mind to. Always try your best and you will persevere! I love you always and forever my little sonshine!

# Gallery

Sean and Papa

Sean & Tito Boyet

Printed in the United States
by Baker & Taylor Publisher Services